THE HAMMER

LEARNING ABOUT TOOLS

David and Patricia Armentrout

The Rourke Book Co., Inc.
Vero Beach, Florida 32964

PHOTO CREDITS
©East Coast Studios: pages 7, 8, 10, 15; © Stanley Tools: title,
pages 12, 13; © Sears, Roebuck & Co.: cover, page 17;
© Armentrout: pages 4, 18, 21

Library of Congress Cataloging-in-Publication Data

Armentrout, Patricia, 1960-
    The hammer / by Patricia Armentrout and David Armentrout.
       p. cm. — (Learning about tools)
    Includes index.
    ISBN 1-55916-121-3
    1. Hammers—Juvenile literature.   [1. Hammers. 2. Tools.]
I. Armentrout, David, 1962- . II. Series.
TJ1201.H3A75 1995
621.9' 73—dc20
                                    94–46472
                                          CIP
                                          AC

Printed in the USA

TABLE OF CONTENTS

A PRIMITIVE TOOL

Tools have been used for thousands of years. Early man made tools with **primitive** (PRIM-et-iv), or basic supplies.

Tools are now made in large factories. Hard woods, metals, and plastics replace the primitive supplies of the past.

One of the first tools made by man was the hammer. Hammers are used for pounding or striking. Today many kinds of hammers are used for many different things.

Native Americans made and used these stone striking tools hundreds of years ago

A CARPENTER'S TOOL

The claw hammer is one of the most common **carpentry** (KAR-pen-tree) tools. Carpenters use the claw hammer to pound or drive nails into wood.

The hammer has a wooden or metal handle. At the end of the handle is a metal head and a 2-prong claw. A nail is struck, sometimes several times, with the head of the hammer.

If the nail begins to bend or needs to be removed, the claw prongs are placed around the nail head and used to pry the nail loose.

Hammers and nails are used when building the frame of a house

NAILS

A nail is a metal **fastener** (FAS-en-er). Fasteners are used to hold materials together. Nails can be found in many sizes. It is very important to choose the correct size nail for the job.

Common wire nails are used most often in wood working. They come in many sizes and lengths. Box nails are thinner and are used to prevent certain woods from splitting. Large wide nails used for heavy work are called spikes.

A construction worker building a
home nails down a section of roof

DRIVING A NAIL SAFELY

By following simple steps for driving a nail, injury to hands or fingertips can be avoided.

Hold the nail with one hand and gently tap it with the hammer to set it in place. Finish driving the nail after removing the hand from the nail.

When driving a nail into wood, pieces or chips of wood may fly into the air. To avoid eye injury, safety glasses should be worn.

Wear safety glasses to protect your eyes when working with any kind of hand tool

Adults should always be there to help children use tools

Professionals work as a team as they do repairs on a front porch

SOFT HEADED HAMMERS

Some jobs require hammers without metal heads. Wooden and rubber **mallets** (MAL-etz) have softer heads.

Wooden and rubber mallets are both used in woodworking, but they each have their own special uses.

Wooden mallets work well when striking plastic handled **chisels** (CHIZ-ulz). Rubber mallets are perfect for positioning brick and stone. Striking plastic or stone with a metal head could cause damage to the materials.

A worker uses a rubber mallet to keep from damaging the thin metal

THE BLACKSMITH

Blacksmith is a name used to describe someone who works with metal and shapes iron. The ball peen hammer is a common tool used by a blacksmith.

The blacksmith heats a piece of iron until it is white hot. After removing it from the furnace, it is placed on an iron block called an **anvil** (AN-vil). The blacksmith uses a ball peen hammer to pound and shape the hot iron into tools, machine parts, horseshoes, and other objects.

Blacksmiths and other craftsmen use hammers that are made especially for iron and metal work

NAIL GUNS

The nail gun, or power nailer, is an electric powered hand tool.

The nail gun has a section that holds many nails. When the gun is placed on the wood, and the trigger of the gun is pulled, a nail is driven with great force into the wood.

Nail guns are used for speed. Carpenters, or woodworkers, can build a house much faster using a nail gun than if they used a claw hammer and nails.

Carpentry work is faster and easier when using a power nailer

OTHER STRIKING TOOLS

There are other basic striking tools common in households. One hand tool is the hatchet. The hatchet has a wooden or metal handle. A sharp blade at the end of the handle is used to chop small pieces of wood.

Another striking tool is the ax. The ax is similar to the hatchet but has a much larger blade and longer handle. It requires two hands to swing it and can be used to split large logs.

The sharp blade on an ax can split large logs with ease

CARE AND STORAGE

Like all tools, hammers need basic care to keep them in good working condition.

Before using a hammer, it should be inspected for damage. Using a hammer with a split handle or chipped head could **mar** (mar) the workpiece or, even worse, injure the user.

After using a hammer, always return it to its storage area. A clean, dry tool box or workbench can store as well as organize tools.

Glossary

anvil (AN-vil) — a heavy iron block used by a blacksmith to help shape metals and hot iron

carpentry (KAR-pen-tree) — the craft of building or doing repairs with wood

chisels (CHIZ-ulz) — metal tools with sharp edges used to cut and shape wood, metal, and stone

fastener (FAS-en-er) — something used to attach or hold materials together

mallets (MAL-etz) — striking tools with large heads that won't harm or damage surfaces

mar (mar) — damage, harm, or spoil

primitive (PRIM-et-iv) — meaning basic, simple, or in the early stages

INDEX